I0559790

SNOWSHOE HARE BEAUTY

![Photograph of a snowshoe hare sitting in grass with a dandelion]

Photos and Poems
by
Dwayne Cole

Parson's Porch Books

Snowshoe Hare Beauty
ISBN: Softcover 978-1-960326-54-6
Copyright © 2023 by Dwayne Cole

All rights reserved. No part of this book may be reproduced or transmitted in any form or by any means, electronic or mechanical, including photocopying, recording, or by any information storage and retrieval system, without permission in writing from the publisher.

Parson's Porch Books is an imprint of Parson's Porch & Company (PP&C) in Cleveland, Tennessee. PP&C is a self-funded charity which earns money by publishing books of noted authors, representing all genres. Its face and voice is **David Russell Tullock** who you can contact at: dtullock@parsonsporch.com.

Parson's Porch & Company *turns books into bread & milk* by sharing its profits with the poor.

www.parsonsporch.com

Preface

Dwayne Cole

The poems in this book were written to create a love for the beauty and wonder of nature in our grandchildren. The nature photos of snowshoe hares were taken and most of the poems were written over the past 12 years in Anchorage, Alaska—Starting when our grandchildren were in kindergarten and first grade.

The book in its present form is intended to be used by parents, grandparents, teachers, and all caregivers of children, as a way of nurturing beauty and wonder.

The poems are appropriate for all ages, but some are clearly written for young children.

> In every person
> a child is hidden who wants
> to dance and play

Many of the poems are in the format of Japanese haiku. The three simple lines of the small haiku, have traditionally been seen as a good place to start teaching children a love of poetry. Haiku uses inspiring nature scenes that enrich the lives of teacher and student. Our grandchildren's art work and poems helped us rediscover a child's wonder in our lives. Seeing the sparkle in their eyes helped us to see with the eyes of a child. The tears of joy washed away some of life's travel stains that cloud our vision.

The wonder of a child blossomed anew in us, becoming fertile ground for tender teachings.

After haiku, sijo is a logical next step in teaching poetry. Sijo is a Korean style of lyrical poetry originally called "short song." Sijo resembles Japanese haiku in having a foundation in nature, but neither sijo nor haiku are limited to nature as subject.

Haiku is a short poem with three lines. The first and third lines have 5 syllables each, the second line has 7 syllables. The syllable count may vary slightly.

The emphasis is on an economy of words.

Sijo has three lines with 14-16 syllables in each line, for a total of 44-46 syllables. The count may vary slightly as in haiku. In sijo, there is a pause in the middle of each line, so in English they are often printed in six lines instead of three.

The natural curiosity of children is contagious. There is a powerful force for change released when children and youth are nurtured in kindness. Keep the spirit of a child in your heart and you will never grow old.

How To Use This Book With Children

1. It is hard to look at the pictures of snowshoe hares without feeling joy and happiness. Let the children have time to express their happiness. You might turn some of the photos into a game of I spy. Do you see what I see?

2. One of the purposes of this book is to teach kindness toward all animals, and especially toward all children. Ask how we can show kindness.

3. Use the book as an opportunity to teach proper use of cameras and photo techniques.

4. You might want to teach color pencil drawing of snowshoes and nature scenes. Our grandchildren loved this activity. As they get older you can move to watercolors and oil painting.

5. My wife and I wanted to teach children to write nature poems. Haiku has been seen as a good way to start this skill. Sijo is the logical next step in teaching children poetry. See the Preface, page 3, for a brief description of haiku and sijo.

6. My books, *Heart Haiku: Alaska Inspired Photos and Poems;* and *Heart Sijo: Alaska Inspired Photos and Poems,* will also be helpful in teaching poetry. These books can be purchased on line from Parsons Porch Books, Amazon, and Barnes & Noble.

7. Let your love of children guide you in finding other creative ways to use this book.

Introduction

Love the animals. Don't deprive them of their happiness.

—Dostoevsky

Snowshoe hares get their name from long and wide back feet, as can be seen in this photo. Their feet work the way human snowshoes do, allowing them to travel easier over powdered snow. Their feet also have fur on the bottom to keep them warm.

Those large feet are attached to very strong back legs. They can jump over 3 feet at a time, and can move as fast as 28 miles an hour.

Snowshoe hares are bigger in size than most other rabbits, and while rabbits dig underground dens and warrens to live in, the snowshoe hare spends all its time above ground, sleeping under bushes, tree stumps, and roots.

Baby rabbits are rather helpless when they're born. They don't have fur, and their eyes are shut. Snowshoe hares are born with their eyes open and have a furry coat. Within a few hours of being born baby snowshoe hares are ready to put those amazing feet to use and start hopping.

Snowshoe hare's large feet also make them good at swimming in the spring and summer. They will jump into ponds and streams to get to food or escape a predator.

Their fur also keeps them warm. It's made up of three different layers. One silky soft layer of fur for insulation, a medium layer of thicker hair, and then a coarse outer layer of hair that sheds. Because of these layers they don't need to hibernate or travel to warmer climates in winter.

Watching the snowshoes play and dance in beauty reveals order and organization in the natural world. Observing this beauty we become one with nature and experience a deep feeling of zestful harmony with all things.

Winter

Letter to Winter

Have you seen my heart,
wrapped in your snow blanket?

Snowshoe, snug in winter coat,
snow from the pure land.

Purity of heart is—
How we treat all with kindness.

(In this Korean formatted sijo, the phrase, "snow from the pure land" is a Korean concept. Teaching sijo poems is a culturally enriching experience.)

Snowshoe hare posing
Can't resist a selfie
New winter fur coat
Will get whiter as snow falls
Better to hide from lynx

(This poem is a Japanese tanka, consisting of five
lines. The first three lines are a haiku. Adding two
additional lines of seven syllables each make it a
tanka. A tanka gives a complete picture of an event.)

D. Cole

Snowshoe Hare Dancing

Winter snowshoe dancing
in sunshine with stocking feet
my winter day treat.

Moves silently
like falling snowflakes
drifting here and there.

Wearing winter fur coat,
a perfect coloration
for hiding from lynx.

However, she still moves cautiously,
rearing up on hind legs
to see if the way is clear,
for kits back home
need her caressing kiss.

Dwayne Cole

Evolution Wonder

I'm a Snowshoe bunny
An evolution funny---

A nose for trouble
Can hop away on the double

Pink tongue to caress my kits
so sweet and tender

Here I sit on a winter day
contemplating life in Alaska.

The day is dark as Prudhoe Bay
black oil spewing out with little light.

I rise to open the drapes
keeping out the seeping Arctic cold.

I walk over to the door,
and feel the bone chilling cold.

Put on skis and glide into the Bog,
to watch the snowshoe at play.

Golden sun peeps over Chugach.
I glide into Spring with kindness.

Spring

Follow the leader
leap from winter into spring
Energy abounding

Dwayne Cole

Love

As darkness moves in
Annual love affair begins
Dancing with great joy

Kicking their heels high
Spring love works magic in snow
Nature is so grand

Bunny Haibun

Nature photo is from my deck.
White winter fur is turning brown.
By the time the snow melts,
coat will match background—
Evolution Beauty and Wonder.

Snowshoe hare skiing,
hopping moguls in sun.
Big feet make good skis.

(Haibun is a literary form in Japan. It combines prose and haiku.)

On a wet snow day,
two little snowshoe hares
came out to play,

Feeling compassion,
I said a prayer for warmth—
Mother, wrap your little ones
In blankets of love.

Snow is melting
Snowshoe hare is molting
Change is in the air

The snowshoes are getting used to me

Sitting in my Cracker Barrel rocker

They hardly pay any attention to me

Lifting my camera to capture their play

It is almost as though they know

I am a friend of animals not a foe

They welcome me with a leap and a hop

Oh the joy of a beautiful spring foray

Photo above taken in April shows molting progress

Molting is shedding
One color of hair to grow new
To match the seasons

D. Cole

Snowshoe hare,
nature's wonders Alaska has to share.
Change color from white to brown
to match the color of their surrounds.
Mother Nature protects her best.
We have to do the rest.
Sitting on rock turning tan for spring,
except for socks.

Eating tender grass
Mother Nature's sweet gift
Be tender with bunnies

Snowshoe Limerick

Once a snowshoe was having fun
Sitting in the early morning sun
Fruit peals are sweet
A very rare treat
Snowshoe says thanks, my hon

(A limerick is a poem with a strict rhyme scheme in which the first, second and fifth line rhyme, while the third and fourth lines are shorter and share a different rhyme.)

Snowshoes are nature's wonders—

Nature's calling card.

Color of fur molts seasonally,

To match the color of the ground.

Expressing the desire to live,

share beauty all around.

Photos of four snowshoe bunnies
playing and silflaying in my yard today.
The term, silflaying, is from one of my favorite
novels, *Watership Down*, by Richard Adams. The
book is a survival and adventure novel about a
colony of rabbits. To silflay is to come out to eat.
The snowshoes in my photos were eating bark from
limbs that had fallen from heavy ice and snow.

Nature Singing

It's spring, the salmon make their way

from sea to spawning glacial streams.

It's May, snowshoes silflaying.

Birds serenade in the silver birch trees.

The Chugach mountains are dancing.

Dark winter becoming all daylight.

It's spring! Snowshoes frolicking.

It's spring! All nature is singing.

These snowshoe hares come into my yard
that backs up to a city park, and entertain me
all year round. It is truly a miracle to witness them
turning from snow white in winter to different shades
of brown. By the end of summer they will be a darker
brown. Except their feet stay white to dance the snow
back in.
They get their name from their large back feet, featured
in some of my photographs.

Snowshoe bunnies
Hopping and stretching
Yoga practice

The lens of my Nikon D750
see this snowshoe better than my eyes.
The camera lens can distinguish
Individual whiskers twitching.

(I Spy, do you see what I see?
Whiskers twitching.)

Many of these poems were written during the COVID-19 pandemic. The title of Alice Walker's book of poems fits the mood of many of my poems—
Hard Times Require Furious Dancing.

Snowshoe hare delight
Kicking up heels in sunlight
Rise join in the dance

Mamma said,
keep my paws clean, hard,
jumping into summer.

Summer

Winter snows have passed.
You can see the last white hairs shedding
and the snowshoe is nibbling
tender green dandelion leaves.
Then the sweet blossom kisses will come.

All nature's seasons
Bring to us the sweetest gifts
Flower blossom kisses

Snowshoe sits quietly
in full brown summer frock.
Munching tender grass.

Photo taken on June 25, 2018.

Nature is Amazing

Doing hip hop
in full brown frock
summer rocks!

I bring a flower
The sweetest I could find
Come and dance with me

Warm day in July
Learning from this snowshoe
Sit and be still

Beautiful summer day
Snowshoes are out to play
Kick your heels high

Snowshoe hare stretch time
Finds its way into my rhyme
I reach for yoga mat

On a rainy day
Snowshoes came in yard to play.
Munching leaves, dancing.
No mortal words were spoken.
Full symphony was singing.

Magic Purple Cloud

In the mystical land of the far North
where Santa and his magical elves live,
colors are spectacular.

The Northern Lights, Aurora Borealis,
can fill the skies with ribbons of
blue, red, purple, green, and yellow.

Magical alpenglow colors transform
mountains, clouds, and trees
into beautiful works of art.

In this magical light, digital cameras,
especially in automatic mode,
love choosing the color purple.

Snowshoe dancing in morning light,
taking on aura of purplish haze,
leaps into mysterious magical realm.

My snowshoe friend,
take me with you—
Let me dance into mystery of fall!

(Photos taken at end of summer, 8-2-2020. in early
sunrise with misty rain.
Red sunlight shining through blue clouds gave
snowshoe a purplish tint
and created the purple haze.)

(For more photos and poems like this one,
see my book, *Alpenglow Miracles: Fire Dance of
Wonder*.)

Fall

The child of wonder in me
thought the children
might enjoy these photos.

Snowshoe Fun

Snowshoe fun for day,
watch me hop with my big feet.
Oops, I slid on leaf!

Look close and you can see the leaf on bottom of
foot.

While at play
Snowshoe leaps away
Shadows can be a fright
In the bright light

Snowshoe in brown fall coat.
Turns from snow white to brown in about 8 weeks,
except feet stay white all year round.

I Spy
Do you see what I see?
Snowshoe hiding from magpies.

Magpies
Dive bombing
Snowshoe

Get away bullies
There are enough bullies in the world
Without some in my yard

When I viewed the pictures I took from my deck
of two magpies harassing a snowshoe hare,
I remembered a 1061 AD ink
and water color on silk painting,
by the Song dynasty master Ts'ui Po
which shows two magpies harassing a hare.

A thousand year old Chinese painting,
shows magpies harassing snowshoe.

German made Nikon camera,
captures game in Alaska.

Putting it in a Korean sijo—
A culture expanding experience.

Snowshoe with fall coat
Will be all Snow White in 6 weeks
Change is adventurous

I'm sitting quietly
Putting my life in focus
One snowshoe at a time

Snowshoe wearing summer brown,
when there is no snow on ground.
Keeps white stocking feet
To dance snow back in.
Then they will put on white coat again.

In nature kindness Matters

D. Cole

Teaching our children to show kindness
to a snowshoe hare is as valuable
to our children as it is to a snowshoe.

I placed this rock in my yard where it would catch
the warm sun rays. My bunny friends like to sit on
the rock when it is warm. I don't know how to define
kindness, but this seems to be a step in the right
direction. Can you think of other ways to show
kindness? See my book, *Kindness Is
Every Step.*

Rays of kindness
Snowshoe sitting on warm rock
Nature smiling

Sound of falling
Snowshoes dash from the garden
Old scarecrow fell down

Snowshoes teach the value of dancing,
kicking up our heels.

We should count it a day lost,
if we do not dance at least once.

The dancer has learned gratitude,
the joy of laughter.

In every person
a child is hidden who wants
to dance and play

*****

grandchildren hopping
more wonderful even
than snowshoes dancing

Molting is complete
Snowshoe nibbling dandelions
Lynx patiently waits

I hesitated to share this photo and the reality that snowshoe hares are the favorite food of the lynx. The first time my grandchildren saw a lynx, they thought it was a large pet with soft fur and golden eyes. "Just a kitty cat" they said. As caregivers we need to teach our children the dangers in the wild. Many wild animals are dangerous to humans, but they are a part of nature's rhythm and beauty.

Snowshoe Play

Enjoying watching snowshoes play.
Watching for awhile I begin to feel,
Nature is looking back at me.

Even magically playing with me—
A little rabbit emerges in the grass.
On the right side of the snowshoe!

Captured Mother Nature's play
on a cold foggy spring day.
Photograph doesn't lie!

Do you remember the "I Spy" books.
Do you see in this photo what I see?
They are both alike but different.
They both have eyes and ears.

Look close at the clump of grass on left side of
picture.

In the melting snow,
snowshoes dancing joyfully.
Oh, happy playmates!

Moving Back to Winter

Snowshoe changing rapidly,
    into its beautiful new coat.

All the better to hide,
    from its enemy, the lynx.

Outside the wind is blowing.
    Let it snow, let it snow, let it snow!

Conclusion

Ode to Snowshoe Hare
(For all caregivers)

Happy little snowshoe bunnies
and their tender days
Touch my heart with love
Tuning me to kinder ways

Beauty and Wonder
Hold communion with the invisible realm
Perfect images of One mind
Tender and Caring

A meditation springs up within me
Feeding on Infinity
The Poet of Beauty and Wonder
Nurtures my soul

Beauty bathed in love is Divine
In this magical experience of cleansing
Truth and Beauty are born from love
and in this matrix fear ceases to exist

Happy little snowshoe bunnies
and their tender ways
Touch my heart with love
Tuning me to Infinity

This snowshoe hare photo is taken from my book, *Kindness Is Every Step.*

In Alaska I have locked eyes with grizzly bears,
male moose with large rack,
and lean and hungry wolves.
One never forgets that feeling of fear.

At the other end of human emotions,
I have had songbirds eat sunflower heart seeds
from my hand on my deck. I have locked eyes with
them and seen the spinning universe.

I have also had snowshoe hares playing in my yard
for the last twelve years. They often came within ten
feet of me, unafraid.
I locked eyes with them and saw Beauty and
Tenderness.

Snowshoes teach value.

Nature moves toward beauty.

Wonder to behold.
We attain value as we protect them.
All living things become valuable.

When snowshoe poses
The beauty of nature
Refreshes my soul

The snowshoes teach me,
it is with the heart that we see.

I see beauty and tenderness
in their springtime dance.

In seeing them as valuable,
I receive value for all people.

Watching the snowshoes playing
I feel an artistic sensation
of something beyond control,
as if someone waved a magic wand.
The creative moment is fresh and new.
I experience an aesthetic moment of novelty. All nature
seems to share in this beautiful rhythmic moment
of mystery and harmony.

This aesthetic moment of creativity gathers the whole
universe, the many, as one, in a dance of becoming.
I dance into a new day with novel possibilities.The
Lynx sits waiting.

BEAUTY AND KINDNESS TRAINING EXERCISE

Poetry of beauty and kindness is relational. Life is about relationships from birth till death. Relational beauty and kindness come naturally in family and community and flows in personal ways. Emphasizing the relational aspects of beauty broadens the definition, moving toward kindness.

Mindfully setting aside times to meditate on how we can better show beauty and kindness can help us become more sensitive and responsive to others within our everyday circles and move to include all persons.

Find a quiet time each day to contemplate on what you desire for your family and yourself:

* To be safe and secure
* To be happy and at peace
* To have good health
* To be free from fear
* To have fun times for all in family
* To see beauty in all people, animals, and all living things

A Summary Vision of Beauty

My vision for the world is that it move toward beauty.
Seeing beauty in nature is a step in that direction.

Beauty is the key for understanding
the loving and generous heart beat of nature.

The inner nourishing of a kind spirit in every person is
one of the most important needs in our world today.

Beauty in one's heart is felt by the universe.

Yet, I am painfully aware of the chasm between this
vision and its ultimate expression in our world that is
so divided.

Visions may be expressed in gentle words,
but they are more powerful when expressed in
tender actions.

Centered in beauty and kindness

We can transform our world.

Snowshoe Miracle

One reason for playing with snowshoe hare
beauties is so the joy you see in them will
become your joy and their beauty will become
your beauty.

The sense of being
one with the snowshoe hare beauty
is Mother Nature's gift.

Snowshoe Hare Beauty is nature laughing
with us, while moving us toward harmony.

BOOKS BY DWAYNE COLE

A Center that Holds: Adventures in Kindness

Alpenglow Miracles: Fire Dance of Wonder

A Prayer of Blessing: As You Go Remember This

A Relational Hermeneutic of Kindness

A Relational Trinity of Kindness

BEARS AND MOOSE OF ALASKA: Nature Poetry

Clouds of Inspiration

Down on the Farm in Georgia: A Poetic Memoir

Dragonfly Magic

Gentle Galilean Glories: The Tender Teachings of Jesus

God and Evil: An Ode to Kindness

Heart Haiku: Alaska Inspired Photos and Poems

Heart Sijo: Alaska Inspired Photos and Poems

Jesus' Transforming Beatitudes: Selected Sermons from Year A

Jesus' Transforming Love: Selected Sermons from Year B

Jesus' Transforming Gentle Teachings: Selected Sermons from Year C

Kindness Is Every Step

Lone Leaf Dancing

Poems Inspired by Process Philosophy

Poet of the Universe: A Vision of Beauty and Goodness.

Rainbows of Hope

Snowshoe Hare Beauty

The Apostles' Creed: A Living Creed for the Living

Church. The Bible: A Poetic Journey

The Book of Revelation: Jesus' Kindness Transforms Suffering

The Serenity Prayer: A Pathway to Peace and Happiness

The Story of the Bible: Authority, Inspiration, Canonization, Translation

TREES AND DRIFTWOOD: Poetic Ecology

When Flowers Speak, Listen

WINGS OF INSPIRATION

www.ingramcontent.com/pod-product-compliance
Lightning Source LLC
Chambersburg PA
CBHW051236120626
46547CB00013B/1664